Constellation

Pieces of Me

Emma Hanks

BookLeaf Publishing

India | USA | UK

Constellation © 2021 Emma Hanks

Presentation by *BookLeaf Publishing*

Web: www.bookleafpub.com

E-mail: info@bookleafpub.com

ISBN: 9789358365405

First edition 2021

To my Mom, thank you for always believing in me.

Acknowledgments

"Thank you to my Dad, for always encouraging my writing and for taking a look at my first drafts before I do anything with them. And also for figuring out the stubborn word that my brain can't think of in the middle of the night.

Thank you to my sister, Abbey, for always helping me out with a bright smile. Well, usually. I appreciate all of your help with wording, all of your patience, and all of your encouragement when I get down on myself. I couldn't have continued this with confidence without you.

And thank you to my friend Avi, for putting up with my continuous spam of poems and giving me useful feedback on every one you read. Your thoughts on them always gave me insight into what I was doing right and what I needed to change to evoke certain emotions and I will forever appreciate your support and encouragement of my writing in all of its forms. "

Preface

"This collection of poems has allowed me to express myself in a way I haven't been able to before. Although some feelings are hard to articulate, I have found that writing has been my outlet, giving me the freedom to discuss the parts of me that are often hidden from others. Emotions and internal thoughts put on paper straight from the heart—a very vulnerable position, indeed.

I chose to write about the aspects of my life that have greatly influenced me in the last few years. The words written here are intended to bring out my feelings from those times or given to me by those people, and I do hope that they are both relatable in some aspects and comforting in others. I hope that some lines will make you stop and think for a moment, about yourself or about what life has to offer.

I have struggled with mental health issues since the beginning of high school and quickly realized that the way I experience mental illness is not the same as the way others experience it. Thus, I chose to express my experience in a way that can be understood. Think of it as one woman's experience, as her two cents on the matter. If you also struggle with your mental health, I hope that you will find some solace here. Remember: You are not alone.

I lost my mother to cancer when I was sixteen. Although it has been nearly four years, I still feel that hole in my heart where her presence should be. The poem titled ""A Letter to My Mother"" discusses my feelings on the matter, something that I have often struggled to do in words, which those around me found quite ironic being that putting things into words is what I'm best at. But loss is a funny thing, it can render even the most articulate people speechless. So, after the letter I wrote to be read at her funeral, this is the first time I have written about her since. However, the letter to her is not the only thing about her in this book. All of these poems... They are my way of communicating to her all of the things that I want her to know about the daughter she left behind. All of the struggles, the good things and the bad—all of it. She may not be able to read them, but it is out there now, for her to see. And I hope that she's proud of the author I've become. She always did encourage me to write for myself. But now I'm writing for the both of us.

So here it is. This... is me. "

1. "Blemish of the Soul"

I'd like to say I'm done with you

And everything that we've been through

But I'm here today

It's not gone away

The damage is done

It's here to stay

A week, a month, a year

Or two

It's still a pattern I can't undo

I'll explain myself until I'm blue

Just like I'd explain to you

It's too late now to take it back

Your words have slipped right through
the cracks

In my skin

In my soul

You'd do anything to have it all

Every day I sit and think

As easy as you'd have a drink

Swallowing down all my flaws

 Just like your bitter alcohol

And though it may be in vain

To completely escape the pain

I'll still endure

Because one thing's for sure

I'll never again love someone like you

Goodbye, so long

It's time we're through

2. "Hands Off"

 Count the seconds until it's over

Count the minutes until the end

Breathe for one, for two, or maybe more

Move the ice-cubes in your hand

Snow isn't black

The summer isn't cold

But you see spots as you shiver

And panic strikes your soul

They don't know what to tell you

When you're staring at the floor

Because even when it's ending

You're always expecting more

You feel them coming often

They're almost a guarantee

And although you try to fight them off

They often bring you to your knees

A hand on your shoulder

Is what they think will help

But how do you tell them with no voice

That you're really beside yourself

Because they don't see how it feels to
you

Their hot hands on your skin

But they're trying their best to help you
out

So you keep the words within

You'll never tell them how it feels

Just let them do their part

But they'll never know how much it hurts

How it's like a vice that has your heart

3. "Flicker"

Raging like flames

Sparkling like glitter

Is it hard to spot my wandering soul?

What about the bad days?

Tracing my skin with the tip of my finger

Do you ignore the girl with the scars?

Blowing kisses to stars

Talking to the moon

I do all the same things a wandering
soul would do

But I'm not the same

With my dark tangled hair

I'm not unique

I'm barely there

4. "**With the Wind of Spring**"

I

    Am like

          A maple tree

I grow where I am planted.

Until

      The wind

           Sweeps up my keys

And I find a new place to flourish.

5. "The Branches that Break"

Branches bend in the wind

They twist and they bend and they break

They might break in two

I'm not a branch, but I'm human

And it's similar—what we go through

A force comes at us

As it always will do

It takes us and bends us

Find our weak points

Then watches chaos ensue

The force is too much

Watch us go on our way

Those weak points get exploited

And nobody stays

They don't care what we say

They don't care what we do

We've lost our battle, try as we may

There's nothing left to do but sit back
and pray

I see the blue sky

And watch it turn gray

Watch the branches in the wind

And they twist and break away

I watch it fly by, like my life gone astray

But I'd never expected this

This life of mine

This runaway

To be like this branch

Broken and frayed

But soaring high

As I sat back and replayed

What I thought was impossible

But was merely midway

I'm not hopeless

Or broken

As many would say

And neither are you

Or anyone who hurts

Or bends

Or breaks

Come this way

The way of the branch as it hurtles away

To a new place

A new place to play

And grow

And stay

A place I'd like to visit someday

But for now I'll build my own

With these broken pieces and frayed
ends

I'll pull my life from the grey

It's not over yet

Not over I say

I'll turn it around and go the other way

To where I can grow

And flourish

And display

All that is gloriously me

Like a branch in the wind

Its freedom at play

Was once broken like I thought I was

But never

Never

Forget

You are free

And alive

And beautiful

And life is better that way

6. **"Fear"**

Fear is what you make of it

It can be helpful

Or a hindrance

Heavy in your chest

Or in your heart

Or light and fluttery

Anticipating what's to come

The tingling in your legs

And ringing in your head

Are there to remind you that you're alive

Alive and feeling

Feeling more

And more

And more

You are more alive in this moment than
the ones before, whether you believe it
or not

It lingers

It rolls over you

In waves

To and fro

An irritable dynamic

An oscillation from sheer panic to a wary
calm

And then back again

This fluctuation

This frustratingly frivolous function of the
brain

Of the body

Of life

It serves no purpose in its present state

It is no help

Why signal danger when there's no
danger to be found?

Why send the brain coursing through
the options it doesn't need?

Forever wondering what might be
around the corner

What if after what if

Scenarios running rampant through your
brain

What else is there to tell?

I feel it coursing through my veins

Buzzing in my head

Tingling in my skin

Fear

Panic

Life

And yet

And yet

I don't know what life would be without it

Without this forever feeling

This weary warning

Wandering through my very
consciousness

Whatever it is now

And whatever it may be in the future

What it is yet to become

I don't know

But I know I'll find out

Someday

Somehow

I'll take back control

And use it for what it's really for

7. "What Am I?"

19

Am I a writer?

Or simply someone looking for a way to escape

To forget their life—just for a little while

Am I an artist?

Or just a girl wishing to see her favourite characters before her

For I cannot see in my mind's eye

Am I a student?

Or just a 20-year-old stumbling down a well-worn path

Searching for a way to make a living

Am I a dreamer?

Or merely an illusion of one

Lofty thoughts that fizzle out before I
can give them the time of day

Am I an activist?

Or a fraud

Challenging my own biases, the
skeletons in my closet

Am I Important?

Or the continuation of a family

By blood and no more

Am I even a person?

Or a figment of some cruel hallucination

A concoction of wind and emotions

Am I what I say I am?

Are you?

8. "The Silence of Night"

The silence of night

Is a gift

Cursed upon me since many years
passed

Fingers on keys

Pencils on paper

The flipping of pages in a book

All of the noises that fill my ears

The rest? Is distant

Cars on the highway

Crickets outside

The baying of wolves

But never another person

Not a single soul

In my house

On the street

In the neighbourhood, it seems

As if I am the only person still up

In the stillness of 4 am

When your thoughts get the better of
you

And no one is awake to help you up
when you fall

When you really are the most alone

In reality while everyone else is in their
personal abyss

A dreamless void

A lucid dream

Chaotic montages of people and voices
in a restless sleep

But you're still there

Sitting

Standing

Maybe laying

But still you are alone

As you always have been

As is takes you away

As it devours you

In the stillness

In the silence of night

9. "Do You Know?"

Do you know that you're worthwhile?

Do you know that you're loved?

Do you know how many people have
wished for you

On the bright stars up above?

Do you realize you're not broken?

As though you're missing parts?

Each one of us is uniquely made

From our souls through to our hearts

Do you see the effect you've had?

All of the lives you've changed?

With your presence and good heart

Please don't let that slip away

Have you told the ones around you?

Have you told them the truth?

Your family and friends all love you

They'll help you make it through

Do you take yourself for granted?

As though it doesn't matter?

I'll tell you now and then again

You deserve to be treated better

Do you realize it now?

How important you really are?

To me, to them, to all of us

Please

Please don't break our hearts

29

10. "Reflections"

Does it hurt you too

When you look in a mirror

Does it pierce your soul like arrowheads

Or scratch your eyes like sandpaper?

Do you stand and stare for hours

Always pulling at loose skin

Your chest growing tighter every
moment

Listening to the monsters from within?

Do you wish to punch the glass

And feel it shatter against your fist

Break it for the way its broken you

Is that also your wish?

Do you scowl when you see yourself?

Both naked and with clothes?

Because nothing can hide what you
despise

Nothing can make you whole

But in truth it's not the mirror I hate

Although it mocks with glee

It is not the dreaded monster itself

The monster itself is me

11.   "I'll Make You Remember Me"

I never thought I'd lose myself to someone else's silence

Never thought it would take me over

Quiet me to a din, never to be heard from again

I was never one to give in

Proud of the stubborn nature my mother had given me

Of all the things she taught me

Of all the things I learned

 How could keeping my truth not be one of them?

Take a step

Take a leap

Take a bound

 Round and round and round

Until nothing was left

But my knees on the rocky ground

The stars may smile at me

But the spaces between mock and taunt

It knows I'm the same

An emptiness between the pretty things

Reaching but never grasping what
should be mine

He knows what he's done

He knows what he's taken

My smile

My love

My faith

Even the bright smile from my face

But he doesn't care

He got what he wanted

The Validation

The Attention

The Praise

But does he realize how worthless they
are

Coming from someone who has none of
those things?

He can't receive what's not willingly
given

Can't keep something I never meant to
set free

My heart may have been his

But my soul was not his for the taking

And I've gone and taken it back

A thief in the night

Plucking what's mine from greedy
fingers

With the flick of my blade

The smile replaced with a sneer

He realizes the mistake he's made

I blare the radio as I leave

A love song to set the scene

He did what he did and I've done what
I've done

Lessons were learned, and I've worked
to come undone

Left behind in my wake

A trail of laughter and tears

He'll remember what he's done to me

For years

And years

And years

12. **"Perpetual Stress"**

It scratches my brain the way it does paper

Begging

Calling

Demanding to be felt

Dulling it doesn't help, it hinders

Hiding it doesn't stop it from finding its way

Its way into my brain

My brain that's already overloaded

Terms

Equations

Diagrams and Exclamations

"Just leave me alone already! Haven't
you had enough?"

It's never enough

It will always keep coming

You can't escape the constraints of a
pencil

Its academic demands

Its devious schemes

Its miraculous methods making me
miserable

Try and try and try again

You won't win

A student is always a student

As a mother is always a mother

Regardless of the status of her child

The habits never leave

Nor the urges

So, keep at it

Ignore it if you must

But know this

The pencil will scratch at your brain too

And reduce your thoughts to dust

13. **"Diamonds Don't Die"**

It gleams on her finger

A beacon in the dark of night

Saving her from the crashing waves of
turmoil

He said their love would never spoil

But what if it did?

What if it already had?

With maggots crawling on her skin, out
of her ears

Over the diamond he boasted he
worked so hard for

What if their desires didn't match?

And it caused a rift between them, a
weed between cobblestones

What if they had never matched in the
beginning?

And she'd acquiesced before seeing
how ravaged she'd become

 The diamond gleamed on her finger

A beacon glinting off the ice

It startled the captain and sent the boat
crashing

The ring still on one bony finger come
the melting of spring

14.   "The Red Button"

I see the button gleaming red

I see the way it looms

A beacon through my foggy head

To help me escape the doom

I see the way it tempts me, calls to me
through the din

I see the way the button tries to coerce
me towards sin

The raging thoughts leave me distraught

Although I fought it was for naught

The red button calls again

15. "To Love a Fictional Character"

They may not be real

                  In this life

                                To
you The warrior, the wizard, the farmer

But they are real

            To me

                  In another

Where I join them on their journeys

And you may not understand

How I could be so attached

So influenced

By words on a page

A face on a screen

A name

A concept

But they have shaped me

    In their own way

        To be the person that I am

As much as the people I can touch

And I love them

    In the same way

        That you cherish a
        childhood friend

As if I've known them all their lives

Because you never forget the people
that saved yours

From the ruins

Of reality.

16. **"Treasures"**

Have you ever seen a movie

That sent shivers down your spine?

That spoke to you in such a way

That it wouldn't leave your mind?

Have you ever read a book

That you've since held so dear?

That no matter what else you read

You come back year after year?

Have you ever met a person

Who saw through to your soul?

Who touched your heart one single time

And left you feeling whole?

Have you ever heard a song

That spoke right to your heart?

And you knew right then and there

That you'd been doomed right from the start?

Have you ever seen some art

That took your breath away?

A painting or a photo

Or a statue made of clay

Have you ever been to a place

That made you stop and stare?

Because you've never felt so at home

Anyplace… anywhere

Would you ever consider

Trying to do your part

So those around you could feel what
you did

And know them all by heart?

Because you'll remember those people

Those places and those things

The words and dancing rhythms

That gave your soul some wings

But don't you dare forget

As you go and walk away

That you could be that person

Make that treasure

That really makes someone's day

17. "A Letter to my Mother"

Dear Mom,

Are you proud of me?

Do you see what I've become

In years one, two, and three?

It may be nearing four now

And I don't know how to feel

I might usually be okay

But how… when you're not here?

Mom, do you still love me?

Even when I've gone astray?

There are things I know you wouldn't
love

Some things you'd even hate

I'm becoming my own person

I hope you understand

But I can't even ask you

Your life didn't go as planned

I missed you at graduation

At prom

Every day

But it's something I must deal with

Your absence

 I wish you could have stayed

This hole in my chest is closing

But it will never disappear

I will always miss you

Now and through the years

I'll miss you at my wedding

But I'll still save you a seat

My kids won't know their grandma

But you'd have the others beat

I'm crying as I write this

Because it hurts like hell

That you're no longer with me

 Our family became a shell

I hope you're up there watching

And loving me from afar

I miss you every day, Mom

You're always in my heart

55

18. **"Abbey"**

I wonder if she knows that I love her

Or what she means to me

I wonder if she realizes

That she's not just family

She may be my little sister

But she's also my best friend

My partner in crime

My confident

Listening right until the end

She's my editor

My hairstylist

And all things in between

My annoyance

And my joy

She's nothing if not unique

You'll always be you

And I'll always be me

So stick by my side

Always

Please

When I'm at school I miss you

And our stupid midnight talks

Random gestures in the hallway

Or a pinch that makes you squawk

We tease

And laugh

And play a part

But know you're always in my heart

You may be only seventeen

But to me know you'll always be

My baby sister

Whom I first met when I was three

I loved you then

And I love you now

So remember what I've told you

On the days you don't know how

19. "Restitution"

Some days I look at myself

And wonder about the deepest parts of
me

About my soul, about my purpose

How I'm drowning beneath the sea

Am I really fit for where I'm going?

To help others in need?

Can I really do that when I myself

Often feel the urge to bleed?

I fit the bill

And think in similar ways

How can I help someone else

When anxiety calls my name?

I do my best to stop it

To bring it to its knees

But it's a roundhouse kick to the face

And the one on their knees is me

Can I really like myself

When all I see is faults

I try and try to fix them

When will it be enough?

Do you see me trying

How I feel compelled?

I want

I need to fix this

To fix this by myself

61

20 "Distortions"

When I look in the mirror

I always see my faults

And I don't mean the ragged looking
human

But what hides beneath it all

The shrill, grotesque monster

That I know hides within

The one that shrieks within my head

The one that always wins

I don't always notice it

It creeps up on me, you see

But I catch it in the rear-view mirror

When I have to let it be

It doesn't matter who I'm with

A partner or a friend

A parent or a sibling

It's all the same in the end

Is it just me overthinking

Or is what I see the truth

Is this thing always lurking

Is that why flames hit the roof

The debris fall down around me

But no one seems to care

Is it that they cannot see them

Am I the only one that's there?

But when I look back on it

Or at my face in the mirror

The reflection that stares back at me

Reduces me to tears

Both inside and outside

I'm ashamed of what I see

And I always wonder the same damn
thing

What do I have to do

To make that monster like me